World Religions General Editor: Raymond F. Trudgian
Formerly Principal Lecturer and Head of the Religious Studies
Department, Borough Road College, Isleworth, Middlesex

THINKING ABOUT BUDDHISM

DAVID NAYLOR

County Adviser in Religious Education for Hampshire

LUTTERWORTH PRESS
CAMBRIDGE

Lutterworth Press
P.O. Box 60
Cambridge CB1 2NT

British Library Cataloguing in Publication Data
Naylor, David, *1935–*
    Thinking about Buddhism. – (World religions)
    1. Buddhism
    I. Title   II. Series
    294.3   BQ4012

ISBN 0-7188-2712-0

First published 1976 by Lutterworth Press
First Paperback Edition 1988

For permission to reproduce photographs 2, 10 and 12 the author and publishers
are indebted to the Sri Lanka Tourist Board and to the Rissho Kosei-Kai for
photograph 16.
The author is most grateful to Dr Gunapala Dharmasiri for taking photographs 4,
13, 14 and 15, to Mr Chandra Wikramagamage for photographs 6 and 17 and to
Mrs Jaini Harris for the charts and map (1, 3, 5 and 9).
The author is also grateful to Mr Chandra Wikramagamage and Mrs Peggy Morgan
for their helpful comments on the text and to Dr Walpola Rahula for permission to
reproduce his translation of extracts from the Pali Canon.

Printed in Great Britain by
St Edmundsbury Press Limited, Bury St Edmunds, Suffolk

CONTENTS

LIST OF ILLUSTRATIONS AND CHARTS

Note

1. In using key concepts from the texts the word in the first instance is given in Pali and Sanskrit. Subsequent references use the term in most common use, for example *nirvana* (Sanskrit) rather than *nibbana* (Pali).

2. Diacritical marks on Sanskrit and Pali words have been omitted.

3. B.C. = before the common era.
   C.E. = in the common era.
   This avoids the use of B.C. (Before Christ) and A.D. (in the year of Our Lord) which presupposes Christian belief.

EDITOR'S INTRODUCTION

The teaching of World Religions has taken a place in religious education in this country for some time. Often, however, it was left until the sixth form when a rapid survey of at least two or three religions per term was made, at the end of which pupils were expected to 'compare' these with Christianity. The most that could be hoped for in such a situation was an acquaintance with the historical founder of a particular faith and knowledge of the more unusual customs and traditions associated with its followers who were thought of as living in some other part of the world.

In recent years the situation has changed so dramatically that a new approach is called for. Not only are many of those faiths now represented in our schools, but mosques and temples form a communal focal point for new immigrants as the synagogues have done for immigrants of another era. Even in areas where the other faiths are not represented the situation presents searching questions through newspaper items and television documentaries.

Long before sixth form therefore a majority of children will have some knowledge of other religions through their own community or the mass media. For an increasing number this knowledge begins in the primary school.

It follows that the school leaver and certainly the student teacher in a college of education will want to look more deeply at a religion other than their own. Ideally at this stage time should be given to one faith only or students could follow a thematic study through the beliefs of the main world religions. Themes such as the nature of God, the meaning of worship, the problem of evil and suffering, war and peace are but a few of the rewarding studies which could be carried out. In this way some approach can be made to another culture, another faith which will provide both understanding and enrichment in preparation for living in the plural society.

This series of 'Thinking about' books is presented with this need in mind. Each deals with one faith only and the text has been prepared by a member of that faith or by Christians of deep sensitivity who have brought their awareness of the religious dimension and their academic training to a presentation of a sympathetic portrayal of another faith.

Not only do they deal with matters of theology and practice but also the social and political implications of each living faith are drawn out for the reader. It is true that we can never begin fully to understand another faith until we have lived for some time in the country where that faith is practised by the majority of people. It is hoped, however, that these books will begin the quest and be related to the search for truth in such disciplines as geography, as we try to understand why particular countries have adapted a certain faith, in history, as we see man searching for an identity often motivated by religion, and in social studies, as we see how mankind has sought to live in meaningful communities.

Apart from its educational value this series is presented in the hope that it will play its part in enhancing community relations in this country. It is some time now since the Rt. Hon. Roy Jenkins (when he was Home Secretary) defined integration as 'not a flattening process to produce "carbon copies" of Englishmen, but equal opportunity accompanied by cultural diversity in an atmosphere of mutual tolerance.'

This book, *Thinking About Buddhism*, seeks to bring that tolerance to the cultural and religious diversity in our society in the hope that whatever the faith of the readers they will understand their own faith at a deeper level as through this book they come into contact with another world faith, and that through their study they will develop a deeper and wider conception of religion.

As Head of Religious Studies in a college of education, and Information Officer for the Shap Working Party on World Religions in Education, I trust that this series will go some way to help the need which is daily expressed in our mail by teachers, student teachers and pupils alike.

Raymond F. Trudgian,
Principal Lecturer and Head of the
Religious Studies Department,
Borough Road College, Isleworth, Middlesex.

AUTHOR'S INTRODUCTION

Learning from Other People's Religion

My own introduction to the study of Buddhism was not through reading a book like this one but through contact with Buddhist monks from Sri Lanka both in England and in their own country. There is no substitute for this if the reader is really to learn and appreciate their beliefs and way of life.

If our quest is to be meaningful and legitimate, we must first recognize the magnitude of the task and look for some signposts to guide the way. This is the purpose of the first chapter.

Secondly we must look at more than one dimension of the religion. Too often the emphasis is purely on belief whilst what the adherents of a religion actually do and how they operate in society is left unexamined. This book attempts to find a balance in this respect. Chapter 4 discusses Buddhist practice especially in Sri Lanka. The final chapter is concerned with responses in the modern world.

Thirdly the reader is asked to avoid premature value judgements and superficial comparisons for the time being and to try to enter sympathetically into another way of looking at human existence.

Fourthly remember that many of the insights propounded originally by the Buddha were the outcome of meditative states of mind which can only be achieved after long and disciplined practice. In the interests of mutual understanding, therefore, we need to recognize that our Western ways of thinking may only be giving us a limited angle of vision on the cosmos and our place within it.

Finally, after making every effort to 'stand in the shoes' of the Buddhist and also pursuing the enquiry beyond the limited scope of this book, the question may be put, 'What does this mean for me?'

David Naylor
1976

SUGGESTIONS FOR FURTHER READING

1. *General Works*
   N. Smart, *The Religious Experience of Mankind*, Fontana.
   T. O. Ling, *A History of Religions East and West*, Macmillan.
2. *For an overview of Buddhism*
   E. Conze, *Buddhism: Its Essence and Development*, Cassirer, Oxford.
   R. H. Robinson, *The Buddhist Religion: A Historical Introduction*, Dickenson.
   H. W. Schumann, *Buddhism: An outline of its teaching and schools*, Rider.
3. *For selections of texts*
   E. Conze, *Buddhist Scriptures*, Penguin Classics.
   E. A. Burtt, *The Teachings of the Compassionate Buddha*, Mentor.
   F. L. Woodward, *Some Sayings of the Buddha according to the Pali Canon*, Oxford.
4. *For the Theravada tradition*
   W. Rahula, *What the Buddha Taught*, Gordon Fraser.
   H. Saddhatissa, *The Buddha's Way*, Allen and Unwin.
5. *For the Mahayana tradition*
   D. T. Suzuki, *Outlines of Mahayana Buddhism*, Schocken Books.
   E. Conze, *Thirty Years of Buddhist Studies* (p. 48ff.), Cassirer, Oxford.
6. *For Zen Buddhism*
   A. W. Watts, *The Way of Zen*, Pelican.
   D. T. Suzuki, *An Introduction to Zen Buddhism*, Rider.
7. *For Meditation*
   E. Conze, *Buddhist Meditation*, Unwin Books.
   Nyanaponika Thera, *The Heart of Buddhist Meditation*, Rider.

Further information and literature can be obtained from:

> The London Buddhist Vihare,
> 5 Heathfield Gardens,
> London W4

1

SIMPLIFIED PERSPECTIVES

Schools of Buddhism

Just as Christianity manifests itself in a variety of forms such as Roman Catholic, Protestant, and Eastern Orthodox, so Buddhism has, during its long history, developed different traditions or schools of interpretation. A simplified view (figure 1) showing only the main schools will be sufficient by way of introduction, followed by an attempt to outline the common ground and to indicate the main lines of divergence.

The evidence for believing that a spiritual genius Gotama (Gautama) Buddha lived sometime in the 6th century before the Christian era is overwhelming. Dispute arises when the attempt is made to distinguish his teaching from subsequent developments, interpretations and embellishments. These key developments are represented in figure 1.

It is generally true to say that Buddhism has shown a remarkable capacity to adapt itself to new cultures and adopt elements which seemed, however indirectly, to contribute to a man's salvation. In Tibet, for example, Buddhism met and adapted to Bonism whilst in China a synthesis between Buddhism and Taoism occurred. In Sri Lanka, however, where Buddhism arrived very early (3rd century B.C. during the reign of the great Indian Buddhist emperor Asoka) it did not meet a strong indigenous culture and the task of uncovering the earliest tradition is easier than it is in areas of greater inter-cultural complexity. As a general rule it will be wise to concentrate on the Theravada tradition of Sri Lanka and from this basis to examine the very important later developments in doctrine and practice.

SCHOOLS OF BUDDHISM

THE BUDDHA

Community of monks

Mahasangha

THERAVADA

11 further schools developed
this tradition
All 12 schools were in
existence by 3rd century B.C.

THERAVADA

Sole surviving school of
this tradition. Sometimes
called Hinayana.*

**Sri Lanka Burma Laos
Thailand Cambodia**

Scriptures:

The Pali Canon

MAHASANGHIKA

5 further schools developed
this tradition
All 6 schools were in
existence by 3rd century B.C.

MAHAYANA

**China Korea Japan
Mongolia Tibet Nepal
Sikkim Bhutan Vietnam**

**Zen Tibetan Nichiren Pure
      Lamaism   Land**

Scriptures:

originally Sanskrit.
Volumes of texts to be
found in Tibetan and
Chinese translations.

* The "small vehicle" carrying
the few to salvation. A
derogatory term used by
opponents

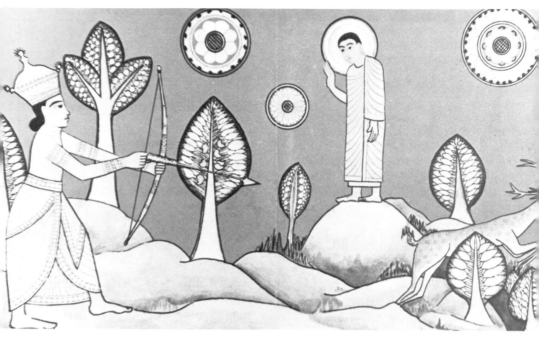

2. Mahinda introduces the gentle teaching of the Buddha to the hunting king Tissa on the island of Sri Lanka in the 3rd century B.C. This is typical Kandyan (Central Sri Lanka) art.

The Scriptures

The situation with regard to the scriptures of Buddhism is complex and there are still considerable gaps in our knowledge. Throughout its history Buddhism has been accretive, it has gathered material like a snow ball on its route through history. This is true even of the earliest documents we possess, that is, they contain early and late material and it is a scholarly puzzle to differentiate between the two. Christianity has a similar, though possibly more manageable task. The Buddha, like Jesus, left nothing in writing. The 'words' of both these founders of great world religions come to us through the communities which they initiated. Jesus probably spoke Aramaic, the New Testament is in Greek. The Buddha probably spoke Magadhi, the earliest texts are in Pali and Sanskrit.

The existence of many schools in early Buddhism has already been mentioned (figure 1). It is highly likely that these early 'schools' had their own canons of scripture. Unfortunately only the Pali canon has survived the vagaries of history as the scriptures of the Theravadins. Scholarly work on translating these texts has made them progressively accessible to the English reader. The Pali texts are not necessarily more original but they provide a useful starting point for study. In general terms the Pali scriptures embody a religion where morality and rationality combine with a humanistic slant. It is these characteristics which appeal to the English reader brought up on a diet of rationalism and empiricism.

The Buddha died in 483 B.C. All the scriptures as we have them go back no further than the beginning of the Christian era. For four centuries the teachings of the Buddha were preserved through group recitation. Buddhists claim that this is a very accurate mode of transmission. By the 3rd century B.C. the scriptures had been classified into five collections according to their topic and approved as authentic. At an important Council in the 1st century B.C. they were committed to writing for the first time in Sri Lanka. The contents of the Pali canon are summarized in the diagram (3).

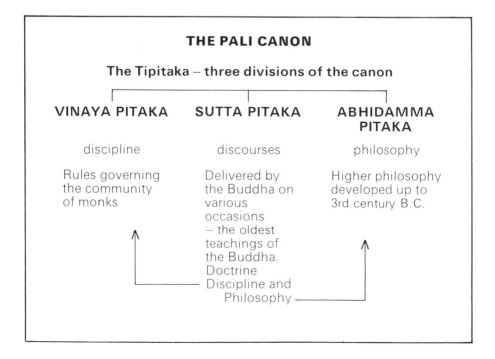

THE PALI CANON

The Tipitaka – three divisions of the canon

VINAYA PITAKA	SUTTA PITAKA	ABHIDAMMA PITAKA
discipline	discourses	philosophy
Rules governing the community of monks	Delivered by the Buddha on various occasions – the oldest teachings of the Buddha. Doctrine Discipline and Philosophy	Higher philosophy developed up to 3rd century B.C.

4. A monk reading the Pali Scriptures.

In addition to this corpus there are commentaries written on the texts contained in the Pitakas, such as Sumangalavilasini on the Digha Nikaya and Samantapasadika on the Vinaya.

The scriptures of Mahayana Buddhism were originally in Sanskrit but very few survived in the original language. Fortunately, however, translations made into Chinese and Tibetan survive in abundance, for example there are 325 volumes of Tibetan scriptures. The quantity of scriptures illustrates the Mahayana theory of developing revelation. The Buddha truth is not seen by them as a closed body of teaching but as a growing corpus.

The Spread of Buddhism

The map on page 17 shows how Buddhism spread from its starting place in Magadha which is marked by the Buddhist wheel symbol. The faith, in general, seems to have spread silently and peacefully without either the violence of the sword or harsh polemic. Buddhism had a tendency to adapt itself to the cultural milieu into which it was transplanted. This, as we shall see, was both its strength and its weakness.

By about the 13th century C.E. Buddhism had disappeared from India. It is interesting to speculate about the reasons for this. It may be that it was not, in its later forms, sufficiently different from Hinduism to constitute a distinctive commitment. At the same time it tended to develop monastic centres which were vulnerable to Muslim invasion from the 10th century.

During the 3rd century B.C., Buddhism flourished under the great emperor Asoka who is said to have sent out missionaries especially to Sri Lanka which was itself to become an important centre of renewal and missionary activity.

By the 2nd century C.E., Buddhism had entered China by way of the silk trade routes. From China the faith spread to Japan by the 6th century C.E. and about a century later it had gained a foothold in Tibet. It is not known when Buddhism entered S.E. Asian countries like Burma and Thailand but it is known that a revival of the Theravada tradition took place there as a result of missionary activity from Sri Lanka about 1200 C.E.

In the 19th century Buddhism began to receive attention in Europe and America. We shall examine this and other aspects of Buddhism in the modern world in our final chapter.

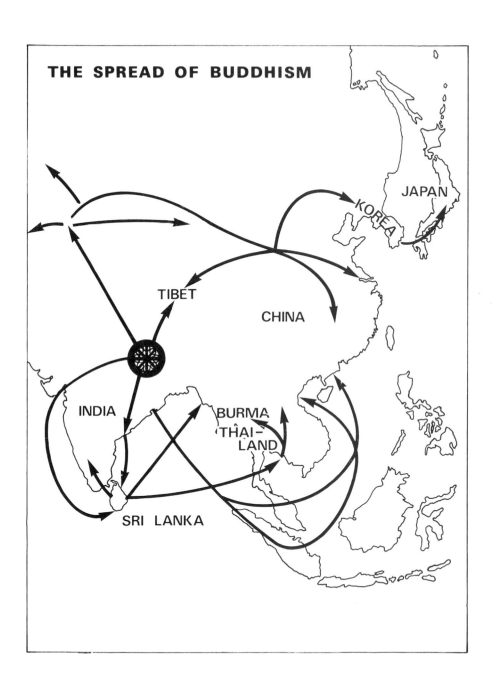

THE SPREAD OF BUDDHISM

JAPAN

KOREA

TIBET

CHINA

INDIA

BURMA
THAI-
LAND

SRI LANKA

2

GAUTAMA BUDDHA

His Life

The 6th century B.C. was of outstanding significance in the history of man's spiritual quest. The Buddha, the great Hebrew prophet Isaiah, the originator of Taoism, Lao-tzu and the founder of Jainism, Mahavira all belong to this period.

The term Buddha is an epithet meaning 'enlightened one'. This title was given to an Indian prince Siddhattha Gotama (Siddhartha Gautama) who belonged to the tribe of Sakya. He is sometimes referred to as Sakyamuni which means saint or wise man of the tribe of Sakya.

The tendency for legends and wonder stories to accumulate around religious heroes is universal. The Buddha is no exception and the accounts of his early life and development are entangled in myth and legend. The word of the Buddha was considered more important than his life and there is no continuous biography in the Pali canon. The simplest outline can, however, be gleaned from the earliest sources. The conception and birth are accompanied by various prodigies. As the Bodhisatta (Bodhisattva) or Buddha-to-be he descended from the higher heaven (*Tusita*) to earth and entered the womb of the beautiful and steadfast Queen Maya without causing her pain. His birth ten months later was honoured by Brahman deities and as a child he showed supernatural powers. His mother died one week after the birth and the father, Suddhodana put the child in the care of his deceased wife's sister. At the age of sixteen Siddhartha married Yasoda and later they had a son, Rahula.

Gautama's life is traditionally depicted as surrounded by princely splendour. He enjoyed a comfortable urban existence as a member of the privileged ruling class. His area of India on the Gangetic plain (northern Bihar and S.E. Uttar Pradesh) was economically expanding and favourable to agriculture. At this time the process of urbanization gave rise to change, insecurity and fundamental questioning about the purpose of life for the individual. In many respects it was a time not unlike our own. It is frequently argued that Gautama was a Hindu but this is rather misleading. At this time, for example, the Hindu tradition as we know it did not exist. Similarly, although he shared in the commonly held belief about rebirth, he did not believe specifically in a creator god or in the efficacy of Brahmin ritualism. Like other mendicant philosophers of his day he sought more satisfactory answers to many of the questions about human existence. His questions are in many respects ours also, whether we accept his answers or not.

The traditional story tells how Siddhartha left the palace against his father's wishes and for the first time met a very old man, a sick man and a corpse on its way to a burning-ghat. Greatly disturbed by this experience he began a process of reflection in a determined effort to solve the riddle of existence. This determination was stimulated by a further encounter this time with an ascetic who was involved in the spiritual quest.

Siddhartha later described to his followers the radical change brought about in him as a result of his experience of the harsh realities of living:

I, too, . . . have formerly . . . myself subject to birth, subject to old age, illness, death, sorrow, defilement, looked exactly for that which is subject (to all that). Then . . . I realized: Why do I . . . who am subject (to all this), seek exactly that which is subject to (this)? Should I not, after recognizing misery in births (etc), search for the unborn, ageless, non-ill, deathless, griefless, undefiled . . . Soon thereafter, young (as I was), having shorn off my hair and beard (and) donned the yellow robes, against the wish of my weeping parents, I went from home into homelessness.

Siddhartha undertook training with two teachers Alara Kalama and Uddaka Ramaputta. After this for six years he led a rigorously ascetic life with five other ascetics. The picture (6) vividly depicts the extent of his self-mortification.

However, in the final analysis, he found both asceticism and the systems of his earlier teachers unsatisfactory. In spite of this he included in his own system elements of mind culture (meditation) which he had learned from the above mentioned two teachers.

6. Siddhartha practising rigorous asceticism prior to his enlightenment.

The Enlightenment Experience

At the age of thirty-five, after six years of asceticism, Siddhartha resolved to sit cross-legged at the foot of a peepal tree until he had attained Bodhi or perfect knowledge. Mara, the Evil One, tried to tempt him to abandon his quest. The battle with Mara is vividly described in the old commentaries and graphically depicted in Buddhist art. The occasion of Siddhartha's victory is accompanied by portents, he is frequently depicted touching the earth which witnesses by means of an earthquake that he is worthy, through previous births, of enlightenment.

Having defeated Mara, Siddhartha remained in deep meditation. In the first watch of the night (6 p.m. to 10 p.m.) he gained knowledge of his former existences. In the middle watch (10 p.m. to 2 a.m.) he attained the power to see the passing away and rebirth of beings. In the last watch (2 a.m. to 6 a.m.) he achieved full knowledge of the destruction of all that defiles or causes suffering and realized the Four Noble Truths. Thus Siddhartha attained enlightenment and became a supreme Buddha at a place now called Buddha Gaya or Bodh-Gaya.

The Buddha remained in meditation for a total of forty-nine days. The story of his decision to teach showed that he realized that the subtlety of his doctrine meant that it would be difficult for people to comprehend. However, he was persuaded by the god Brahma to teach for the benefit of those who could understand. In the Deer Park at Isipatana (modern Sarnath near Benares) he gave his first discourse to the five ascetics who had been his companions earlier. He outlined the Middle Way between the extremes of self-mortification and self-indulgence. His teaching ministry lasted forty-five years during which time his chief disciples were Sariputta and Moggallana and his personal attendant the monk (*bhikkhu*) Ananda. The Buddha taught Brahmins and outcasts, rich and poor, literate and illiterate. Within the community he formed (the *Sangha*) the usual caste barriers were not binding.

The Buddha's Death

The Buddha's death (*parinirvana*) is important in several respects. Since, according to the Pali texts, he made no claims to divinity and discouraged reliance on supernatural forces, his death could be regarded simply as the death of a great teacher. The deep reverence felt for him by his disciples could not accept this in any realistic sense. This is shown first in the protest made to his master by Ananda when he realized that the Buddha proposed to die in a relatively insignificant place, Kusinara (Kusinagara). The offensiveness of the idea of an obscure dying place

7. The famous Samadhi Buddha statue (circa 3rd century C.E.)
Anuradhapura, Sri Lanka.

8. The *parinirvana* of the Buddha, Polonnaruva, Sri Lanka.

suggests that this story may well be based on historical fact since fabricated accounts would tend to be more elaborate out of reverence for the enlightened one. The Buddha had previously told Ananda, '. . . it is in the very nature of all things near and dear to us to pass away . . . how can it be that such a being (as the visible Gautama Siddhartha) should not be dissolved'. On his deathbed the Buddha's last words were, 'Transient are conditioned things. Try to accomplish your aim with diligence.'

The bare historical facts about the end of Siddhartha's life are that he died like any other man and that his death occurred in comparative obscurity. After his cremation the process of glorification began with the distribution of his remains as relics for veneration. As such they were treated like those of a king and placed in burial mounds or *Stupas*. The hero, now viewed through the eyes of faith, was said to have borne the thirty-two major marks and eighty minor marks of a great man. The net result is that he is sometimes honoured by believers in the same way as gods are honoured in other traditions (see Chapter 4).

Previous Buddhas

The Western observer of Buddhist art is sometimes baffled by cave paintings and carvings showing several Buddhas. How is this to be related to the historical Gautama Siddhartha who is a familiar figure in world history? The answer is to be found in the Buddhist idea that time should be considered in two senses: historical time measured in years and cosmic time measured in aeons. The notion therefore arises, even in the Pali canon, that other Buddhas appeared in previous aeons. Sometimes seven Buddhas are mentioned and occasionally twenty-four.

Gautama Buddha's Previous Lives

The Buddha born in historical time, Siddhartha Gautama is believed to have begun to prepare himself for Buddhahood many aeons ago under his twenty-fourth predecessor, the Buddha Dipankara. At this time it is said that he was a learned Brahmin called Sumedha who, out of reverence for the Buddha Dipankara, cast himself on the muddy ground as a carpet for the Buddha to walk on. On seeing this gesture Buddha Dipankara predicted, 'You shall be young Brahmin, in a future period after immeasurable and incalculable aeons . . . a fully enlightened Buddha . . . what I am now you will become one day.'

It is consistent with the Buddhist world view and in keeping with their doctrine of the Buddha that an incalculable period of time would be necessary to develop the perfect qualities of a Buddha. The *Jataka* stories recount how the Bodhisattva (Buddha-to-be) developed the ten perfections: charity, morality, renunciation, wisdom, energy or effort, patience, truth, determination, love and equanimity. They describe in many episodes how the Buddha-to-be gave away all he had or sacrificed even his life for others. When they are recounted in Buddhist countries these beautiful stories act as encouragement towards the spiritual development of the seeker after enlightenment.

The Future Buddha

Just as Gautama Siddhartha is not to be seen as the first Buddha neither is he to be regarded as the last. Buddhists predict that at some future time another Buddha will appear. The name given to this future Buddha is Metteyya (Maitreya). At present he is believed to be a Bodhisattva in the *Tusita* heaven but in the distant future he will be born in this world and bring many to enlightenment.

Mahayana Buddhology

At risk of oversimplification we have traced the development of thinking about the Buddha through several phases:
1. The death of the human Buddha at Kusinara.
2. The cremation of his body and the distribution of relics.
3. The transfiguration of the historical facts through the accumulation of legends.

4. The elaboration of the perspectives in which the Buddha is viewed:
   a. as having accumulated all perfections in his previous existences as told in the *Jataka* stories.
   b. as being only one of a line of Buddhas who appear through cosmic time.

Theravada Buddhists have tended to retain the humanistic perspectives whilst at the same time accepting that his life pointed beyond itself to the spiritual *dharma*. The Buddha is reported as saying, 'What is there in seeing this body of mine? Whosoever sees the spiritual *dharma*, he sees me; whoso sees me sees the spiritual *dharma*.' The Mahayana tradition carried this process of stressing the transcendental and supramundane perspectives even to the extent of populating the heavens with Buddhas and Bodhisattvas. The Three-Body Doctrine, which is relatively late, provides a structure within which these ideas can meaningfully be related.

The Three-Body Doctrine

In the Mahayana tradition we find an effort to understand the importance of Gautama with reference not only to his earthly ministry but also in the perspective of final truth. In this he is set in cosmic time side by side with the other Buddhas and Bodhisattvas who are even said to be as numerous as the grains of sand on the banks of the Ganges. An attempt to understand their significance in the human as well as in the absolute spheres is systematized in the Three-Body doctrine.

This theory tries to reconcile the earthly and the cosmic notions by holding that behind all Buddhas lies the Buddha nature or *dharmakaya*.

The word *dharma* has many meanings but primarily it means the natural law or cosmic order which underlies the world. It was this eternal *dharma* which the Buddha perceived, personified and materialized in his teaching. It is in this context that the designation of the Buddha as *Tathagata*, literally meaning 'He who thus came', should be understood. The twenty-four Buddhas and the future Buddha Maitreya all have in common the *dharmakaya*, the first of the three bodies. As the absolute reality the *dharmakaya* defies description. Most sutras conceive it as impersonal but some suggest more personal attributes with special stress on compassion.

The second of the three bodies is designated *Sambhogakaya* (body of bliss). This refers to the transcendent dimension of a Buddha who can be experienced spiritually but not through the senses. Amida (Amitabha) is a very popular example of a transcendent Buddha who assists beings towards liberation through rebirth in the heaven known as Pure Land.

The Three-Body Doctrine

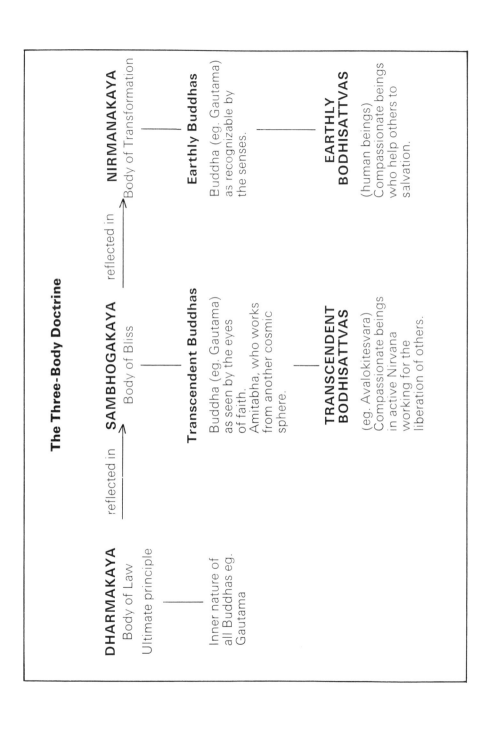

DHARMAKAYA
Body of Law
Ultimate principle

——— reflected in ———▶

SAMBHOGAKAYA
Body of Bliss

——— reflected in ———▶

NIRMANAKAYA
Body of Transformation

Inner nature of
all Buddhas eg.
Gautama

Transcendent Buddhas

Buddha (eg. Gautama)
as seen by the eyes
of faith.
Amitabha, who works
from another cosmic
sphere.

Earthly Buddhas

Buddha (eg. Gautama)
as recognizable by
the senses.

**TRANSCENDENT
BODHISATTVAS**

(eg. Avalokitesvara)
Compassionate beings
in active Nirvana
working for the
liberation of others.

**EARTHLY
BODHISATTVAS**

(human beings)
Compassionate beings
who help others to
salvation.

Buddhas who, like Gautama and Maitreya, appear or will appear in the world of men do so in human form. This human form is designated *Nirmanakaya* (body of transformation) and is used to describe the Buddhas who have been and will be visible to the normal senses. The function of the earthly Buddha is to teach the *dharma*.

From the Western perspective the earthly Buddha tends to be regarded as most important. To the believer, on the other hand, the underlying Buddha nature is central and the *Sambhogakaya* or body of bliss which can only be experienced spiritually is an important focus.

These developments in the doctrine of the Buddha from the cult of a human hero through idealized superhuman notions to metaphysical forms should not be seen as alien parasitic growths attaching to an otherwise 'rational' and 'this worldly' Buddha. Great religions have the quality of evolving deeper levels of understanding because of the potency of the embryo which gives them birth.

Some cautious comparison with Christian doctrine may assist our understanding of the Three-Body doctrine. The Buddhist scholar Suzuki says:

> If we draw a parallelism between the Buddhist and the Christian trinity, the body of transformation (*Nirmanakaya*) may be considered to correspond to Christ in the flesh, the body of bliss (*Sambhogakaya*) either to Christ in Glory or the Holy Ghost, and *Dharmakaya* to Godhead.

The parallel should not be pressed too hard because the framework of thought is different, but from the point of view of developing doctrine we can say that the Three-Body doctrine and the Trinity doctrine are playing in the same league.

Mahayana Buddhists take the view that the *Sambhogakaya* can be perceived in every spiritual leader such as Muhammad, Jesus, St. Francis, Confucius and others. As with the Hindu doctrine of Avatars these ideas can lead to a very wide tolerance amongst Buddhists.

3

HOW GAUTAMA BUDDHA TAUGHT

We must begin our summary of the key teachings of Buddhism with some important preliminary observations. Gautama's *method* of teaching is illuminating as well as the substance of his teaching. If the reader examines some Pali texts from the sutta pitaka (canon of discourses) he will find an introductory formula such as: 'Thus have I heard . . . the Blessed one was living at . . .' This is then followed by a discourse which is carried through in a characteristically logical manner.

The style of argument used in these discourses shows that Gautama was concerned about the opinions, abilities and presuppositions of his hearers. Gautama is not only depicted as having preached sermons but also as one who skilfully led his hearers from the known to the unknown in discussion. Similarly the listener is encouraged to test the truth of the claims made in his own experience. Gautama is said to have visited a place called Kesaputta where the people were confused by the variety of religious teachers making competing claims to have the truth. Gautama offers them the following piece of advice:

Yes, Kalamas, it is proper that you have doubt . . . for doubt has arisen in a matter which is doubtful. Now look you Kalamas, do not be led by reports, or tradition or hearsay. Be not led by the authority of religious texts, nor by mere logic or inference, nor by considering appearances, nor by delight in speculative opinions, nor by seeming possibilities nor by the idea, 'This is our teacher'. But, O Kalamas, when you know *for yourselves* that certain things are unwholesome and wrong and bad then give them up . . . and when you know *for yourselves* that certain things are wholesome and good, then accept them and follow them.

This advice should not be interpreted purely rationally, that is, paying attention only to demonstrable and verifiable knowledge. The category of experience for the Buddhist is much wider. It includes meditative states of mind accessible only through the practice and development of spiritual intuition.

In the light of these basic stances Buddhism claims to be a 'come and see' faith (*ehipassiko*). The invitation to 'come and see' is extended to all. Gautama did not have the 'closed fist' approach. His teaching was for all; nevertheless both he and his followers have always accepted the idea that teaching needs to be adapted to the spiritual and intellectual capacity of the listeners. This idea is known as 'skill in means' (*upaya*) and there are many examples of the way in which Gautama used it.

One appealing example concerns a young monk who was trying hard to meditate but who was all the time crying because he was in love with a beautiful girl from his home village. Gautama was told about the young man and when he saw him he promised that if he meditated diligently Gautama would give him five hundred more beautiful girls. At this the young monk meditated with such zeal that he achieved the goal of *nirvana* and had no more attachment to the world.

This basically pragmatic approach has influenced the development of Buddhism as it was transplanted into different cultures. Like Gautama himself, those who carry his message into new cultural contexts, instead of dismissing the indigenous ideas of their hearers, used *upaya* to direct these ideas gradually towards Buddhist goals. This approach has given Buddhism a tolerant attitude and to the student of religion some fascinating examples of cultural adaptation.

The Four Noble Truths

The task of unravelling 'original' Buddhism is extremely complex. The texts contain early and later material (see Chapter 1) and subsequently cultural adaptation has occurred. The net result is that, if a Buddhist is asked about the basics of his faith, he may give a variety of answers. Certain key stances, however, are evident and these can best be seen by means of an examination of the Four Noble Truths. These truths were expounded in Gautama's first 'sermon' given in the Deer Park at Sarnath, near Benares. They are best understood as a diagnosis of the human condition followed by a prescription for transcending it and can be summarized as follows.

1. We are in a state of anguished impermanence.
2. This is caused by grasping which takes us from one state to another.
3. This grasping can be stopped.
4. The eight-fold path is the key: A Middle Way.

The First Noble Truth

The word which has been translated as 'anguished impermanence' in the above summary is *dukkha*. It has a deeper meaning than the English words can capture. There are three interconnected aspects of *dukkha*. The first is the notion of impermanence. All conditioned states are subject to change, nothing in the ordinary life of man is permanent. The second aspect is sometimes translated 'ill' or 'suffering' and arises on account of impermanence. Suffering arises, not only out of unpleasant states of affairs such as sickness, misfortune and death but also on account of pleasant and happy states when separation from such states occurs. We sometimes refer to this latter state as 'anti-climax' and it occurs after joyful events such as birthdays and Christmas. It is important to note that Gautama did not deny that there is happiness in life and in relationships but he realistically pointed out their transitoriness.

The third aspect of the first truth of Buddhism is the most difficult one to grasp for the Western mind. The notion that behind the changing form of man's outer life there lies a permanent and abiding soul or self is deeply embedded in the human consciousness. Gautama denied the existence of such an entity in his doctrine of no soul. Human personality according to Gautama consists of what are called the five aggregates (which are, matter, sensation, perceptions, mental formations and consciousness). These, Gautama argued, are all slowly burning themselves out and have no permanent core. The Fire Sermon in the Sutta Pitaka vividly drives home this point.

The analysis of human existence contained in the first noble truth as impermanent, suffering and lacking in a permanent soul will probably strike a cord in the reader's own experience. Threats to peace of mind occur, not only in our own lives, but on account of our knowledge of the sufferings of other men. Easy and rapid communication in a shrinking world has sharpened our awareness of the fragile nature of existence. Does this analysis make Buddhism a pessimistic religion? Buddhists claim that it is neither pessimistic nor optimistic but realistic and that the facts must be faced in order to make way for the positive aspects of the message. This positive aspect is to be found in the third and fourth noble truths. The movement of thought is from realism to hope.

The Second Noble Truth

This truth follows the diagnosis with an analysis of the causes and origin of anguished impermanence. Suffering and the continuity of beings in the cycle of existence (*samsara*) is brought about by craving (*tanha*). In the words of Gautama's first sermon:

> The noble truth of the origin of suffering is this: It is this thirst (craving) which produces re-existence and re-becoming bound up with passionate greed. It finds fresh delight now here and now there, namely, thirst for sense pleasures; thirst for existence and becoming and thirst for non-existence.

Thus, factors which cause becoming and birth into the unsatisfactory round of *samsara* are identified in Buddhist psychology with a view to eliminating them. Three important roots of new mental formations are greed, hatred and ignorance. The occurrence of birth or re-becoming is dependent on the fundamental law of *kamma* (*karma*). *Karma* means action through the will and can be either good or bad. The basic assumption is that the law of cause and effect operates in the universe. Hence, good actions and thoughts cause good results; bad actions and thoughts cause bad consequences. Thoughts, as well as actions, act like radiation according to Buddhists, and both thoughts and actions can be compared to a boomerang; their return is inevitable. The important point to grasp is that even good *karma* produces craving because it may involve clinging to life as if there were some permanent element within it. But, as we have seen, Gautama believed in no such entity, not even a soul.

A question about this aspect of Buddhist thought usually springs to minds reared in a different culture. This concerns the problem of rebirth without a transmigrating soul. The answer is best given in the form of an analogy. If a billiard ball is struck with a cue the impulse given is transmitted to the next and subsequent balls. A portion of the ball is not transmitted but the original strike gives rise to subsequent events and determines the direction of them. Within this kind of framework death simply means that the physical body decays, the life force is believed to continue and produce another birth. Thus, for example, suicide is no solution to the problems of life since it merely means the end of the physical body.

The objective of destroying the *karmic* roots of birth is central to Buddhism. As we shall see in the following chapter many Buddhist practices are intended to bring about the destruction of craving little by little. Craving for, or clinging to, life is the same as clinging to death according to Buddhism. The secret must lie in the destruction of craving.

The Third Noble Truth

The third truth assures the believer that clinging to phenomenal existence can be eliminated. The term used for the cessation of suffering is *nirvana* which literally means 'blown out' — the end of the process of becoming. The analogy of quenching fire is sometimes used. The idea is that the fire goes out when there is no more fuel in the form of craving. *Nirvana* is a mystical state beyond description in words and hence direct statements about it are avoided. Negative terms such as extinction of thirst, unconditioned, cessation, extinction, are considered more appropriate. Though negative words are used to describe this state, *nirvana* is understood also in a positive sense. One word which, however inadequately, conveys this positive aspect is 'peace'. The term generally used for one who has destroyed the roots of becoming is an Arahant (Arhat). Reference is also made in the Pali canon to *nibbuta* man meaning one who has become 'cool'. Gautama himself is the archetype of the ideal man. Like Gautama, the Arhat achieves the mystical state of *nirvana* in his lifetime. In such a man the mental and physical aggregates still exist but are no longer associated with clinging and, on his physical death, no individualized person would remain. The goal of the ideal man seems to have been central in early Buddhism. The notion of *nirvana* as a transcendent state is there also and both aspects were capable of interesting development as Buddhism grew.

It is important to note that the emancipated or 'cooled' mind does not become a dormant non-entity. If this were the case Gautama himself and the Arhats who have followed his path would have been apathetic individuals unconcerned about anything after attaining liberation. Instead, they show in their example, that when the mind is purged of greed, hatred and ignorance it is transformed and can act with unselfish compassion.

The Fourth Noble Truth

The final truth contains the prescription necessary for attaining the state of *nirvana* or 'coolness'. It is outlined in Gautama's first sermon in these words,

> And what, O monks, is the noble truth of the way that leads to the cessation of suffering? It is the noble Eightfold Path, namely, right understanding, right

thought, right speech, right action, right livelihood, right effort, right mindfulness and right concentration.

This path, Gautama explained at the beginning of his sermon, is the middle way between the extremes of self-mortification and self-indulgence. It outlines the practical means by which *nirvana* can be realized.

The eight aspects of the Path are interrelated and intended to be cultivated simultaneously according to the capacity of the individual. Thus, for example, right understanding is only possible if right mindfulness and concentration are practised. For the purpose of exposition we shall examine them in the traditional order.

Right understanding involves the understanding of things as they really are, that is, as explained in the Four Noble Truths. In this context, understanding is not simply a question of intellectual grasp but requires deep penetration into ultimate reality. Such understanding is only possible when the mind is free from impurities and fully developed through meditation.

Right thought requires the development of the noble qualities of love and non-violence to all living beings and the rejection of selfish desires and ill-will. Right speech, right action and right means of livelihood are to be interpreted in relation to Buddhist ethical principles. They are closely connected with *the five precepts* which are the moral foundation of Buddhist practice. These precepts, which all Buddhists, whether monk or layman, undertake to follow are frequently listed as restraint from (1) killing (2) stealing (3) sexual misconduct (4) lying (5) drinking intoxicants or taking drugs. In his book *The Buddha's Way* Dr Saddhatissa has re-translated the five precepts from the Pali and shown their much wider meaning and significance:

1. I undertake the rule of training to refrain from harming living things.
2. I undertake the rule of training to refrain from taking what is not given.
3. I undertake the rule of training to refrain from a misuse of the senses.
4. I undertake the rule of training to refrain from wrong speech.
5. I undertake the rule of training to refrain from taking drugs or drinks which tend to cloud the mind.

Understood in the light of this translation, the precepts can serve as an aid to self-examination and self-criticism. The precepts are to be interpreted, not as a call to asceticism but as a call to examine thoughts and actions and their consequences. Sense pleasures are to be seen for what they are and enjoyed but not abused.

10. Moonstone, Polonnaruva, Sri Lanka.

The sixth aspect of the Eightfold Path is usually translated right effort. This is mainly concerned with the will; through control of the mind, unwholesome states are to be rejected and wholesome states developed. The result of such control will be good *karma* and the reduction of craving.

The remaining two factors, right mindfulness and right concentration are directly concerned with control of the mind through meditation. It is the quality of mindfulness which makes many Buddhists attractive and considerate people. The control resulting from awareness of every action, thought and word gives the quality of serenity and calmness to the good Buddhist personality. This is a difficult quality to describe, it is best understood when encountered in people. The subject of meditation will be dealt with in the next chapter.

The moonstone and the eight steps at Polonnaruva, Sri Lanka graphically depict the teaching of Gautama outlined in this chapter. The moonstone

11. Moonstone and steps at Polonnaruva, Sri Lanka.

is not merely decoration but is symbolically linked with the steps and Buddha image (see photo 11). The eight steps symbolize the path to wisdom as embodied in the Buddha. The jutting out moonstone reminds the devotee of the nature of existence. The outer ring depicts the flames of passion to which all beings are subject. The band of animals represents the four perils of existence: birth, disease, old age and death. The leafy creeping plant symbolizes desire. The geese represent wise men who turn away from the cycle of existence and rise above it by way of the Eightfold Path to transcendental wisdom which is symbolized by the Buddha image.

Buddhism: A Way of Liberation

As the teaching of the four holy truths illustrates, Buddhism is essentially a religion of liberation. Human life as we know it is seen as ultimately unsatisfactory and therefore to be transcended in some way. It is for this reason that Gautama refused to pronounce on questions of a speculative nature if he considered them to throw no light on the pathway to liberation. A Buddhist story tells of a monk named Malunkyaputta who refused to lead the holy life until certain questions about the origin of the universe, the nature of man and life after death had been answered. Gautama is said to have responded in the form of a parable:

> Suppose Malunkyaputta, a man is wounded by a poisoned arrow, and his friends and relatives bring him to a surgeon. Suppose the man should then say, 'I will not let this arrow be taken out until I know who shot me; whether he is Ksatriya (of the warrior caste) or a Vaisya (of the trading caste) or a Brahmana (of the priestly caste) or a Sudra (of low caste); what his name and family may be; whether he is tall, short or of medium stature; whether his complexion is black, brown or golden; from which village, town or city he comes. I will not let this arrow be taken out until I know the kind of bow with which I was shot, the kind of bowstring used; the type of arrow, what sort of feather was used on the arrow and with what kind of material the point of the arrow was made.

The point is well taken. Whatever the standpoint taken on such questions the facts of birth, life, death, and the practical questions about how to achieve ultimate happiness remain.

This overarching concept of liberation led Gautama to use the analogy of the raft in another of his parables which concludes with the words: 'I have taught a doctrine similar to a raft — it is for crossing over, and not for keeping a hold on.' The objective is not merely to explain the world or to retain the teaching for its own sake but to cross the surging ocean of *samsara* to reach the ultimate goal of *nirvana*.

A similar analogy is used to designate the two main schools of Buddhism (see Chapter 1). The term Hinayana, originally a derogatory term, literally means 'the small vehicle (or raft)' which, its opponents alleged, carries only a few to liberation. The term Mahayana, on the other hand, the school which began about the beginning of the Christian era as the second phase of Buddhist thought, means the great vehicle (or raft) which claims to carry a wider range of human types to liberation. The two schools have much in common but it will be useful here to highlight their differing views about the way to achieve liberation. Since Theravada is the sole surviving sect of the so-called Hinayana school its teaching will serve to focus on the differences.

36

The Way of Liberation in Theravada Buddhism

Theravada Buddhism could be labelled 'transcendental humanism' in that it teaches that liberation can be attained by human effort. Gautama achieved enlightenment and this is the basis of his authority. He can show others the way but the effort to walk the Eightfold Path is left to the follower. The goal of enlightenment or *nirvana* can be achieved by both men and women, those who attain it are called Arhats.

The Ways of Liberation in Mahayana Buddhism

The monastic ideal of early Buddhism and the goal of arhatship (sainthood) gradually lost their potency mainly because of lack of appeal to the laity on whom the *sangha* depended for its support. Probably as a result of social interaction with the laity new forms of Buddhist belief and practice began to emerge. The result was a broadening of the means by which the ideal of liberation was thought to be achievable.

Most potent in this process was the development of the Bodhisattva as the ideal figure. Such a being, destined to become a Buddha, postpones his entrance to the bliss of final *nirvana* (*parinirvana*) out of compassion in order to lead others to liberation.

The Bodhisattva's Vow

However innumerable sentient beings are, I vow to save them!
However inexhaustible the defilements are, I vow to extinguish them!
However immeasurable the *dharmas* are, I vow to master them!
However incomparable Enlightenment is, I vow to attain it.

This new ideal had great appeal to all kinds of people whatever their social or intellectual status. Furthermore it could easily be justified by reference to Gautama Buddha himself. Gradually both Buddhas and Bodhisattvas were seen also in a mythological way as celestial beings (see Chapter 2).

The Bodhisattva, whether earthly or celestial, is seen by Mahayana Buddhists, to be one who can be called upon to help a being to liberation. Hence, in addition to the way of self-discipline developed in the earliest phase, the Bodhisattva's way is added. A transcendent Bodhisattva who is a particularly popular helper to liberation, according to a later development of the Mahayana, is Avalokitesvara of whom it is said:

. . . Happy are those beings in the world, who remember his name: they are the first ones to escape samsaric suffering.

Similarly Amida (Amitabha) Buddha who is believed to dwell in the cosmic paradise called the Pure Land helps those who call upon his name to achieve rebirth there. The Pure Land is a beautiful place where the conditions for achieving *nirvana* are very favourable.

The Bodhisattva way brought in its wake other ideas about the path to enlightenment. First there is the development of a matriarchal strain within the Mahayana tradition. Wisdom is depicted as a female Bodhisattva. Second it is possible to see the introduction of magical ideas into popular belief as the laity became increasingly important. This development led in turn to the idea that cultic action or the chanting of mantras can lead to emancipation. These mantras are Sanskrit words or phrases with mystical connotations.

The drive towards liberation can also be seen in the growth of ideas about the future Buddha Maitreya. Fervent hopes of emancipation are encouraged by the thought of being reborn in the distant future under the Buddha Maitreya and thereby achieving release from *samsara*.

The rise of Ch'an Buddhism in China (Zen in Japan) beginning about 500 C.E. can be seen partly as a reaction against the multiplicity of means of salvation being propagated within the Mahayana tradition and partly as the result of interaction with Taoism. Zen Buddhists wished to return to the spiritual life rather than to images and rites and they advocated a simplification of the approach to enlightenment. As the way to enlightenment, Zen emphasized meditation. One important Zen school taught that enlightenment occurs suddenly like 'a flash of lightning'. Another school made use of koans, paradoxical questions or riddles meant to lead the seeker away from logical processes of thought to unspeakable or paradoxically expressed truths.

At the end of this survey of Buddhist teaching and its development we return to the centrality of the notion that experience of enlightenment, and not words about it, is the aim. The multiplicity of Buddhas, Bodhisattvas, the volumes of sacred scripture, the images, the mantras and other cultic formulae are, like the raft, dispensable once the true point of the teaching has been experienced. As Professor Ling has said: 'The welter of words in Buddhism is a testimony to the ultimate inadequacy of words.'

4

WHAT BUDDHISTS DO

In our account of what Buddhists do we must be selective. The ritual and ceremonial aspects described in this chapter refer in particular to practice in the Theravada tradition in Sri Lanka and have been chosen to throw light on the doctrinal matters raised in previous chapters.

The Sangha

The community of monks originally established by Gautama Buddha himself is the body responsible for propagating and preserving the teaching (*dharma*). Entry into the *sangha* often takes place when a boy is very young. He becomes a novice, has his head shaven and wears a robe which is usually orange but can be yellow. As a novice he learns about Buddhism from the monk who gives him lower ordination or, more often, he attends a monastic school known as a pirivena. At the age of twenty or more he is granted higher ordination and becomes a bhikkhu (monk), after ten years he is dignified by the title Thera (or elder) and after twenty years he becomes a Maha Thera.

The average Westerner's picture of the Buddhist monk is of a solitary figure intent, rather selfishly, upon achieving his own salvation. In practice monks play a variety of roles in society and differ accordingly in the goals they set themselves. Many monks live at village temple sites with two or three other monks; they are involved in preaching, teaching and social work amongst the community and, in return, are supported by the people. The traditional daily begging round is not very widely practised today in Sri Lanka, instead the monks are supported on a more organized

12. A young monk.

rota basis. In addition to helping people in their day-to-day living, some monks express their social concern through active involvement in politics (see Chapter 5). Since entry into the monastery takes place usually in boyhood, it is not surprising that monks vary in the goals they set themselves. There are forest-dwelling monks who live apart from society in order to concentrate on meditation with the goal of *nirvana*. Such monks are greatly revered by the general population. On the other hand there are monks who, through involvement in works of compassion, seek to acquire merit for the achievement of a better rebirth. The goal of *nirvana* for such a monk is more distant.

The Three Refuges and the Precepts

Monks and laymen alike take on the precepts. Monks are required to live in accordance with the 227 rules of the Vinaya (see Chapter 1). The most frequent act of laymen is to say the three refuges. These are chanted in Pali and can be translated:

Worship to the blessed Arhat truly fully enlightened
I go to the Buddha for refuge
I go to the *dharma* (doctrine) for refuge
I go to the *sangha* (the order) for refuge
(repeated three times)

This is followed by repeating the five precepts (see page 33). Monks and pious laymen (upasaka) and laywomen (upasika) take on eight precepts. This usually occurs on poya days which are quarter days of the lunar month considered holier than the rest. In the eight precepts the third is changed so that all sexual relations are renounced and the following three are added:

I undertake the precept to abstain from eating at the wrong time.
I undertake the precept to abstain from dancing, singing, music and shows and from wearing garlands, perfumes, from finery and adornments.
I undertake the precept to abstain from high beds and big beds.

In practice this means not eating solid food after midday, abstention from entertainment, and sleeping on mats on the ground. Monks undertake ten precepts. This involves splitting the seventh into two and adding:

I undertake the precept to abstain from accepting gold or silver.

The Temple

A typical temple site in Sri Lanka incorporates several features. First the *Pansala* which is the living quarters for the monk or monks. It is here that the monk(s) study, meditate and freely receive people needing their help or making offerings to them.

Besides the *Pansala* there is normally a *Bo tree* as a symbol of enlightenment, a *Stupa* or relic mound, a building housing a Buddha image and a *preaching hall*. Buddhists visit the Temple site on poya days to make offerings usually of flowers but sometimes of incense, lights or food. These offerings, known as Buddha puja are normally made at a small shrine in the home. The Buddha image is the usual focus for offerings but they are also made to the *Bo tree* or the *Stupa.*

Buddha Puja

When a layman or monk makes offerings at the *Bo tree*, *Stupa* or Buddha image he says two Pali stanzas:

Flowers

This heap of flowers, which has colour and scent
I offer at the sacred, lotus-like feet of the Noble sage

I make offering to the Buddha with these flowers
And through this merit may there be release
Even as these flowers must fade
So my body goes toward destruction.

Incense

To him of fragrant body and face, fragrant with infinite virtues, to the Buddha I make offering with fragrant perfume.

Lights

With this lamp which shines brightly, destroying darkness I make offering to the truly enlightened lamp of the three worlds, who dispels the darkness (of ignorance).

It will be recalled that the orthodox Theravada doctrine holds that the Buddha is a dead human being and not a living deity. If it is the case that the Buddha is powerless to help, why make offerings to him? The orthodox answer is that the offerings are not made to gain favour but they serve to develop pure thoughts in the mind of the devotee. In focusing his

13. Paying respects to the Buddha at a wayside shrine and Stupa.

thoughts on the good qualities of the Buddha he acquires merit by destroying the roots of craving — greed, hatred and ignorance.

Food
Food is offered with the words:

May the Lord accept this food from us taking compassion on us.

This translation of the Pali stanza suggests that the Buddha is being asked for help. The practice may well have been influenced by Hindu customs. However, unlike the Hindu, and consistent with the orthodox doctrinal stance, the Buddhist does not consume the food as a means of access to divinity but discards it for consumption by dogs or beggars. As with other types of offering, the orthodox belief is that the intention behind the action is to cleanse the offerer's mind by means of good thoughts.

Funerals
Birth and marriage in Sri Lanka are purely civil functions but funerals are accompanied by ritual which throw interesting light on the doctrines described in Chapter 3.

Funerals are occasions when the mourners can be reminded of the impermanence of life. Monks therefore preach sermons on the *dharma*. Such sermons normally involve quotations from the Pali canon with some exposition. In addition to the normal recitation of the three refuges and the five precepts, two further ritual actions of interest for our purposes occur.

First the coffin is covered with a cloth which is symbolically taken by the monks for the *sangha*; as it is being taken those gathered say:

I give this corpse-clothing to the *sangha* of monks.

The monks reply with the words:

Impermanent indeed are all compounded things . . .

Secondly water is poured into a cup until it overflows whilst the monks chant in Pali:

As water rained on a height reaches the low land, so indeed does what is given here benefit the dead.

At certain fixed intervals after the funeral (usually seven days, three months and one year) the bereaved give meals to the monks and the merit acquired by such a deed is transferred to the person who has passed on by means of the symbolic pouring of water. With all these ritual actions the important point to bear in mind is that the intention of the doer is central, the more unselfish his actions and thoughts the more he develops spiritually.

Festivals

Wesak

At the full moon day in May at the festival of Wesak, Buddhists celebrate the birth, enlightenment and death of the Buddha. This is a temple-based festival and the Buddha puja activities mentioned earlier are performed. In addition there are processions with music and colour. Like Christmas, Wesak is a time for giving presents and decorating homes especially with lighted candles or lamps.

Tooth-relic Procession

The significance of relics has already been mentioned. The relic provides a bridge between the Buddha and the devotee in the sense that the Enlightened One is regarded as present in the relic. On ten nights leading up to the full moon in August each year a great procession of a tooth relic of the Buddha, believed to have entered Sri Lanka in the 4th century, is carried in an elaborate casket on the back of an elephant. The procession is accompanied by acrobatic drummers and officials in colourful costume. The occasion has become a great tourist attraction. Although the tooth-relic temple is not an official place of pilgrimage, attending the perahara is regarded as meritorious and many Buddhists attend from all parts of the island.

Poson

This festival takes place on the full moon of Poson (June) especially at Mihintale in Sri Lanka to commemorate the first arrival of Buddhism to the island. King Devanampiya Tissa met Ven. Mahinda at Mihintale on that day and this was the beginning of Buddhism in Sri Lanka.

Asala (Asalha)

On the full moon day of Asala (July) a festival is held to celebrate three important events: Buddha's conception in his mother's womb, his renunciation and the occasion of the proclamation of the First Sermon to the five ascetics in the Deer Park near Benares.

14. Tooth-relic Temple, Kandy, Sri Lanka.

Meditation

Meditation is central in Buddhism and the experience resulting from its practice is more important than intellectual assent to doctrines. If the reader wishes to 'come and see' Buddhism some experience of meditation will be necessary.

Meditation is recommended for both monks and laymen, though the life-style of monks is recognized as being more conducive to such practices. Buddhists recommend that the aspirant needs a teacher to prescribe appropriate practices in the light of his own experience of the path and according to his pupil's character and capacity. They also stress the need for discipline (setting aside appropriate time and place for example) and the fact that there are no short cuts to genuine meditation.

The subjects prescribed for meditation are very varied and extensive according to individual types of character. Examples could be the Buddha and his qualities, the *dharma* and its profound clarity, the *sangha* and the qualities embodied in it. Further examples might be the body or death. Loving-kindness is a very important focus for meditation. In this practice the meditator is instructed to think thus:

> Let not one deceive another nor despise any person whatever in any place. In anger or ill will let not one wish any harm to another.
>
> Just as a mother would protect her only child even at the risk of her own life, even so let one cultivate a boundless heart towards all beings.
>
> Let one's thoughts of boundless love pervade the whole world — above, below and across — without any obstruction, without any hatred, without any enmity.

In any form of meditational practice the first essential is calmness and tranquillity. The most common aid to the development of what is usually called mindfulness is to concentrate on breathing:

> (The meditator) sits cross-legged, keeps body erect, establishes mindfulness before him and breathes in and out mindfully.
>
> Breathing in a long breath, he knows, I am breathing in a long breath . . . or breathing in a short breath he knows, I am breathing in a short breath . . .

Mindfulness can carry over into routine daily activities:

> (The meditator) when walking, knows, I am walking, or standing, knows I am standing . . .

The development of mindfulness can cultivate an inner tranquillity which helps to give a new perspective and, for the adept can lead to higher states of consciousness or ecstatic trance.

Another important practice involves the development of insight. Here the meditator, so to speak, observes closely the activities of his mind and body. When disturbances whether internal to the mind or body or external in the environment occur, he analyses them with increasing accuracy. The outcome in experience is a more acute self-awareness, increased control of the mind and emotions and a growing insight into the world as it really is.

5

BUDDHISM IN THE MODERN WORLD

Important questions about the future of religions in the rapidly changing world are not easily answered. A consideration of the present status of Buddhism in certain key geographical areas will provide interesting data on the subject. The reason for this is that in China and South East Asia Buddhists have found themselves in a stark encounter with communism whilst in Japan they have met the most intensively industrialized society in the world. The impact of Buddhism and Buddhist scholarship in our own country is no less interesting and this will be the subject of some concluding observations.

Buddhism in Theravada Countries

Sri Lanka can legitimately claim to be the mecca of the Theravada tradition. Today it has a population of about twelve million, democratic government and the highest literacy rate of Asia. In the past Sri Lanka was subject to three streams of foreign conquest: the Portuguese (1505–1658), the Dutch (1658–1796) and the British (1796–1948). Independence from the British was achieved in 1948 and subsequently political power was assumed by the Singhalese-speaking Buddhist population.

If the traveller drives around Colombo or any other part of the beautiful island he will be confronted by large numbers of Buddha statues, many of them modern and of considerable size. It is abundantly clear these images have become the visible public symbols of Buddhist nationalism. This method of expressing national identity by reference to the ancient Buddhist culture has involved some interesting changes.

15. A typical street scene in Kandy, Sri Lanka showing Stupa and shrine.

In the *sangha* the role of some monks has changed. At the heart of Buddhism, as we have seen, there is the ideal of renunciation. This has remained the ideal and the ascetic monk is greatly revered by the general Buddhist population. However, in the contemporary situation, monks are increasingly involved in political and social affairs. This concern with worldly affairs has resulted in mixed roles; they are both symbols of renunciation and of Singhalese Buddhist political nationalism at the same time.

An important Buddhist national leader of modern Sri Lanka, Anagarika Dharmapala, who founded the Mahabodhi Society in 1891 for the renewal of Buddhism, began a new movement which sought to resolve the tensions in the Buddhists' new role. He advocated the possibility of renouncing the world whilst living in it by becoming an *Anagarika*. The Anagarika has a special vestment, a white robe symbolizing world renunciation but, unlike the monk, his head is not shaven and this symbolizes his greater involvement with the world. In such a person the traditional role of the lay Buddhist of merit-making through compassionate involvement in social interaction and the traditional role of the renunciate are combined.

Some of the more traditional Buddhists have reacted to the fact of open political involvement on the part of monks by saying: 'we respect the yellow robe but not the person'. The patched robe and the begging bowl are symbols for what they regard as Buddhist. There is, however, another way of looking at the problem. Liberation, as we saw earlier, is central to Buddhism and this concept can be interpreted in a wide sense. The Buddha is said to have refused to teach the *dharma* to a man who had been working without food all day, until he had been given a meal. The monks with him on this occasion grumbled whereupon the Buddha is reported to have said: 'If I preach law (*dharma*) while he is suffering from pangs of hunger he will not be able to comprehend it . . . Monks, there is no affliction like the affliction of hunger.' The account of this incident in the Pali canon is followed by a discourse on moderation in eating.

From this episode we can see how it can be argued that spiritual liberation is not possible if the minimum conditions for bodily welfare are absent. Since provision of an environment conducive to spiritual growth involves political action, many monks feel justified in espousing political causes. In such a role they are regarded by many lay people as credible sources of advice despite the tensions involved in the ambivalence of their role. Some monks adopt 'right wing' stances but most fit the label 'left wing'. Others, of course, find Marxism a viable solution to this-worldly problems. In Sri Lanka, however, they are more insulated from direct confrontation with Marxism and it is to Burma and China that we must turn to examine the full implications of this encounter.

In Burma where the proximity of Maoist China sharpens the debate, the story is rather different. Burma is exposed to Communist infiltration. The population is 84 per cent Buddhist and organized Burmese Buddhism, although it supports the socialist ideal of the welfare state, has nevertheless opposed the Communist ideology.

The premiership of U Nu is important because, as a devout Buddhist, he supported the faith in general and the *sangha* in particular. He was responsible for initiating the sixth World Buddhist Council in Rangoon which began in 1954 and ended in 1956. Addressing parliament in 1948 he declared:

> In the case of men who believe in the Four Noble Truths, the most urgent duty is to attain *nirvana* in the shortest possible time . . . Property is meant not to be saved, nor for gains. It is to be used by men to meet their needs in their journey to Nirvana.

On another occasion in 1950 he stated,

> When a Marxist makes the statement that Karl Marx possessed great wisdom, we have no reason to argue with him. But when he invades our realm and ridicules the Lord Buddha . . . then it is our duty to call him down . . . the wisdom or knowledge which can be ascribed to Karl Marx is less than a tenth of a particle of dust lying at the feet of our great Lord Buddha.

In a variety of publications coming from Burma and other Theravada countries the contrasts between Marxism and Buddhism are stressed. Thus, for example, whereas Marxists see materialism as an end in itself Buddhists see it only as a means to a greater end. Marxists it is argued see the world in terms of a closed system of natural physical laws whilst Buddhists believe in *karma* which is not restricted to present existence. The whole concept of class struggle is seen by Buddhists to be incompatible with the Buddhist ethic of non-violence and the motive of destroying hatred. For Marxism social reconstruction depends on social and economic legislation, for Buddhism social action can only result from individuals who have first controlled their own minds. The two ideologies are seen also by Buddhists to differ in method. Marxism, they claim, depends on propaganda and compulsion whilst Buddhism, taking its example from the Buddha himself, relies on persuasion and rational argument.

In spite of this polemical literature, there are sufficient points of contact between Buddhism and Communism for it to be possible to conceive of a Buddhist Communism. The Buddhist scholar, Vijayavardhana writing in Sri Lanka, points out the affinities between Buddhism and ideal communism (as opposed to its political realization in Russia and China) in the following terms:

> The early *sangha*, as established by the Buddha comprised real communists whose precept and practice have virtually disappeared from the earth. They were a classless community, every member of which was equal . . . (they) owned no property, all possessions being held by the community . . . Communism, in its orthodox theoretical form, is thus not at all inconsistent with the communism of the early *sangha*.

Both confrontation and compromise will no doubt continue into the future; the ultimate outcome is difficult to predict.

China
The official position with regard to religion in Maoist China was origin-

ally stated by Mao himself in 1945 and subsequently codified as article 88 of the 1954 constitution. It states:

> All religions are permitted in China's liberated areas in accordance with the principle of freedom of religious belief. All believers enjoy the protection of the People's Government so long as they are abiding by its laws. It is the peasants who put up the idols and, when the time comes, they will throw the idols out with their own hands . . . it is wrong for anyone else to do it for them.

The liberalism of these statements is more apparent than real. In fact in China the life blood of Buddhism, the *sangha*, has been the subject of ruthless attack. About 200,000 monasteries and temples that once dotted the land were converted to other uses after 1949, only a small number remaining as museum pieces. At the same time life for the 'unproductive' monk is almost impossible. The need to abide by the laws has given room for further persecution. Large gatherings of people are against the law and this makes many Buddhist festivals impossible. Similarly day-to-day ritual activities such as offering food to the Buddha are spurned as wasteful.

These activities indicate that Buddhism in its traditional form involving doctrines, literature, art, *sangha*, ritual and meditation will probably gradually disappear. Does this mean the end of Buddhism in China? Some Buddhists take an optimistic view and argue that Maoist goals of beautifying the land and unselfishly working for the common good are the same as Buddhist goals. They would go so far as to argue that Chinese people, especially Mao, who are capable of great unselfishness in sacrificing personal ambition for the common good are really Bodhisattvas. The public slogan 'Put the public welfare before one's own' could be seen to exemplify the Buddha mind. In these circumstances, the optimists assert: 'The Policy of Mao Tse-tung is Buddhism.'

Other Buddhists would however see the situation differently. The subordination of everything to increased production and the satisfaction of physical needs they see as a denial of Buddhism. The cultural revolution has not eliminated the religious needs of man, the need for purification, for the mysterious and the transcendent. National days to boost the will to produce can be no substitute for the 'otherworldly' dimension of a Buddhist festival. The results of cutting people off from customs developed over centuries will eventually break through.

A revival of Buddhism in its traditional form seems highly unlikely in China but the elements of Buddhist belief and practice which satisfy deeply felt human needs are unlikely to remain suppressed for ever.

Japan

Japan with a population of 100 million embodies all the characteristics of a rapidly changing, complex industrialized society. The social ferment created by modern technology is accompanied by a fascinating array of religious and quasi-religious responses. The culture of Japan is an interesting mixture of Buddhist, Confucian and Shintoist elements all of which are apparent both in everyday life and in the new religious movements.

The new religions of Japan present interesting data especially to the sociologist of religion. These new communities are involved in the total way of life of their adherents. They provide a pattern of security in a context of anxiety and fear of the unknown. Their message is usually simple and positive and in addition they provide recreational, educational and medical facilities. It will be sufficient here to focus on two sects which claim Buddhist roots.

Soka Gakkai is the largest modern Japanese sect. It claims to have thirteen million followers. The name Soka Gakkai means 'value-creating academic society' and, though it was founded in 1931, its origins go back to Nichiren (1222–1282). Nichiren was a fiery scholar and prophet who claimed that absolute truth is to be found in the ancient text known as the Lotus Sutra. He expressed this idea in a positive and popular way by means of a formula. *Namu Myo-Horenge-Kyo*, Reverence to the Wonderful Truth of the Lotus Sutra. The chanting of this formula in faith, he proclaimed, would bring about unity with the supreme Absolute and with the Buddha. At a time of uneasy government Nichiren's fierce nationalism and positive faith met with success. Its aggressive and intolerant spirit, however, was very un-Buddhist and its links with orthodox Buddhism were tenuous.

The Soka Gakkai sect stands in the Nichiren tradition and has a similar nationalistic and militant flavour. It uses well organized and effective propaganda to gain followers and is involved as a right-wing political party in the Japanese parliament. Followers are encouraged to direct all their efforts towards the coming millennium.

Rissho Kosei-Kai is a modern popular expression of Mahayana Buddhism. The photograph (16) shows the 'Great Sacred Hall' which is the headquarters of the organization. The activities of the sect range from medical services to education and recreation and therefore, as with the Soka Gakkai sect, there are many social reasons for joining.

A very important activity of the sect is group counselling. These sessions known as 'hoza' occur daily in groups of ten or twelve with a leader. In these sessions problems and difficulties are discussed by refer-

16. The Great Sacred Hall of the Rissho Kosei-Kai in Tokyo.

ence to the four noble truths and the Eightfold Path. They are helpful to people living under the stressful conditions of urban industrial Japan.

England

When European scholars introduced Buddhism into the West during the 19th century they based their view of it on the scriptures of the Pali canon. Their early contact with this body of writing appeared to them to reveal a religion based purely on reason without either a personal God or revelation. This is still the picture given in many books on the subject but gradually the religious and mystical elements of Theravada as well as Mahayana Buddhism were brought to light. It was gradually realized that Buddhism not only involves rationally based expositions of doctrine but also contains a rich store of legend and story. It also embodies a highly developed non-verbal element involving meditation and ritual practice intended to encourage the living of the holy life.

The earliest Buddhist influences in this country came from Theravada countries especially Sri Lanka and this still holds true today. Within this tradition a strong element of rationality and evidence of scientific ways of thinking can be found. There are several reasons why this element of the teaching was emphasized. On the one hand European scholars tended to be searching for a religion based on reason and so were selective in their treatment. On the other hand they were themselves influenced by Buddhist

17. East meets West to celebrate Poson at the London Buddhist Vihare.

scholars who, under colonial influence, were seeking to justify their own tradition in the light of Western thought forms. Another reason could be that, in accordance with Buddhist missionary techniques, these Eastern scholars were practising 'skill in means' in finding linking points in the host culture. It is interesting that, since the rape of Tibet by the Chinese, Tibetan Buddhists are finding refuge in England. Their tradition with its rich mythological and magical elements may move the influences in a more mystical direction and find listeners in the present generation.

The Future of Religion

The impact of Buddhism on the cultures we have examined may provide some pointers to the future of religion. Buddhism, whilst showing a concern for 'this-worldly' welfare, has at the same time resisted the idea that the establishment of a purely materialistic society is an end in itself. Our study of Buddhism reminds us that man not only manipulates his world in ingenious ways but also seeks to transcend it. In so doing he asks questions about meaning and purpose in life and finds himself confronted by the inescapable facts of ageing, transitoriness and death. At this point he can listen with profit to the insights of religious men. He will find in the Buddha's Middle Way a realistic diagnosis of his condition and a prescription for living worthy of his practical consideration.